FLINT—THE VERSATILE STONE

BY

H. J. MASON

ILLUSTRATED BY

H. DE CAUX

PROVIDENCE PRESS,
Providence Place,
Wardy Hill,
Ely,
Cambridgeshire.

ISBN 0 903803 01 1

Cover Picture:

'Pony' Ashley at mouth of his mine 1931

Photo—Norfolk Museums Service (Thetford Museum)

CONTENTS

‘A nodule of flint is a geological memoir, an introduction to botanical ecology, a palaeozoic treatise, a geographical and industrial grammar of prehistoric man, a road-itinerary, a mining manual, a course in the technique of Roman mural construction, a chapter of mediaeval aesthetics, an extract from ecclesiastical history, a digest of the development of local genius, a tractate upon the line of division between ancient and modern, a fairy-tale and a local guide-book.’

From ‘Remembrance’ by H. J. Massingham.
(By permission of the publishers B. T. BATSFORD LTD.)

FOREWORD

Knapping flints is the oldest industry known to man. From the time that Stone Age man first learned to work with flints to produce a range of implements and weapons, there has always been a demand for flints for one purpose or another. When the Bronze Age dawned, metals began to supersede stone for many purposes but it was not until 1832 when the 'lucifers' were developed, that flint strike-a-lights first began to be replaced as a reasonably simple means of starting fires.

In historical times flint has been used extensively for building, as an ingredient in glass and pottery manufacture, and in flintlock guns. Comparatively recently, methods have been developed for using calcined flints mixed with cement to produce decorative panels and cladding for internal and external use on buildings. Similar material can be used for road surfaces to improve light reflection and to increase tyre adhesion. Gun-flints are still manufactured by the firm of H. Edwards of Brandon in Suffolk.

During my research for this book I have had help from a large number of people who responded to my letter published in the *Eastern Daily Press* and magazines. To all of them I acknowledge my thanks. I would also particularly like to thank the following:

Norfolk Museums Service (Thetford Museum) for permission to reproduce drawings made at the Ancient House Museum, Thetford. Also the Curator, Miss A. J. Maddock, for her interest and help.

Mr. R. A. Copeland of the Cheddleton Flint Mill Industrial Heritage Trust, Leek, Staffordshire, for permission to reproduce the diagram and explanatory information from his book 'A Short History of Pottery Raw Materials and the Cheddleton Flint Mill'.

Miss N. Walley of the Walley Group, West Thurrock, Essex, for information on the present day industrial use of flint.

Director of the Glasgow Art Gallery and Museum for permission to take and reproduce the photographs of the firearms which are displayed in the Museum.

Mr. Jim English for information on flint knapping; and

Mr. H. de Caux for his illustrations.

Every effort has been made to trace copyright owners of photographs. Acknowledgements are given, where known, and further acknowledgements will be given in later editions if copyright holders contact the publisher.

Wardy Hill,
ELY.

H. J. Mason,
March 1978.

1. INTRODUCTION

Man is known to have existed in Europe for at least 400,000 years. For most of this time his survival depended largely on his ability to make stone implements. At the dawn of the early Bronze Age, about 4,000 years ago, for the first time it became possible for metal tools to be manufactured and only then did the importance of stone implements begin to diminish.

During his evolution, early man acquired the ability to walk upright, which left his forearms free for purposes other than movement. He must have discovered that fragments of stone held in his hands helped him to do tasks for which his hands alone were inadequate or unsuitable. Fragments of stone with sharp edges were useful in cutting vegetation, shaping wood, butchering animals required for food and for scraping fat from hides which could then be used for clothing and shelter. At some stage man also discovered that by striking certain stones against each other, sparks could be produced and fire kindled.

The use of tools gave him superiority over other animals and eventually time could be spent on leisure and other cultural pursuits rather than in a continual search for food and the bare necessities of survival.

Wherever there were flints, it was possible to find pieces with razor-sharp edges which could be used to satisfy the needs of the early Stone Age man. This supply was not inexhaustible and did not provide anything other than the crudest tools.

These difficulties were overcome by shaping tools from stones, which could be flaked by striking with another stone used as a hammer. The very earliest man-made tools are difficult to distinguish from naturally occurring flakes but over many centuries skills were improved. Different cultures developed and are still recognised by the way in which they made their tools.

Flint was found to be particularly good for stone implements as it had natural lines of fracture, could be polished smooth and a fine cutting edge could be produced.

There were two basic ways of making implements from flint. Either a hammer stone was used to break fragments off the piece of flint to gradually work the core into an axe, sickle blade or something similar, or flakes were broken off and from them spear heads, arrow heads and a variety of other delicate tools were made.

The first axes were held in the hand but eventually systems of hafting were developed, including boring a hole through the axe head so that a shaft could be fitted. Early flint axes were left just as they were made from the core but later, smooth axe heads were made by polishing and grinding them against harder stones.

Apart from using hammer stones for tool making, Stone Age man was also skilled at using sharpened sticks of wood for pressure flaking. This enabled

Stone Age hand axe

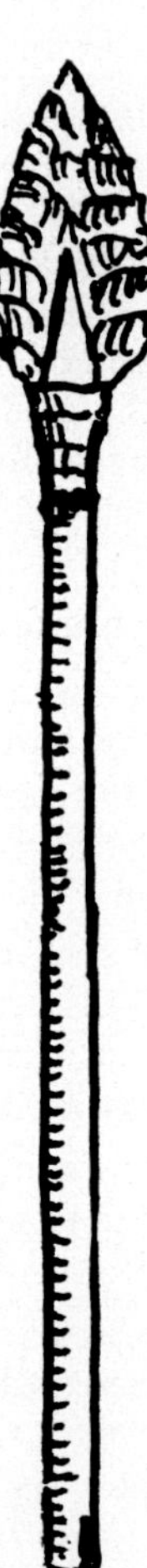

Stone Age arrow

him to make very fine flakes into arrow heads of various shapes and sizes. The flake was first worked into the approximate shape and size and then, by applying pressure with the aid of the stick, small flakes were dislodged from the surface and edges. This skill was acquired again during the early part of this century by knappers who used the technique to reproduce 'Stone Age tools' and other ornamental flint objects. In this way, Bill Basham made an alphabet and a necklace in flint.

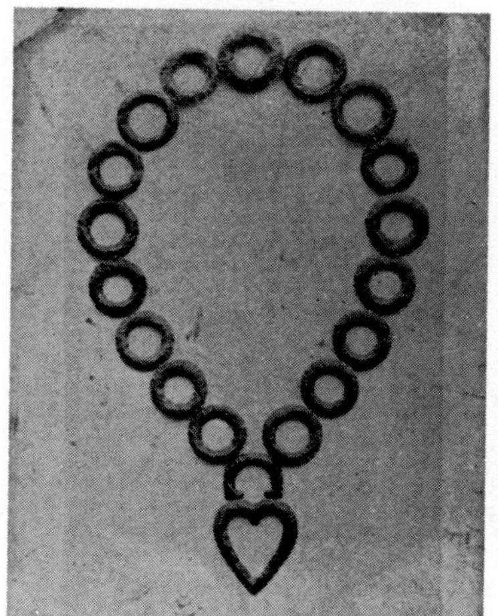

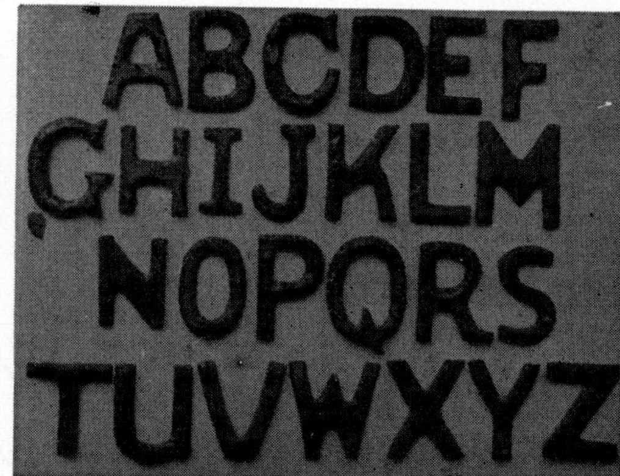

Flint Necklace and Alphabet
made by Bill Basham

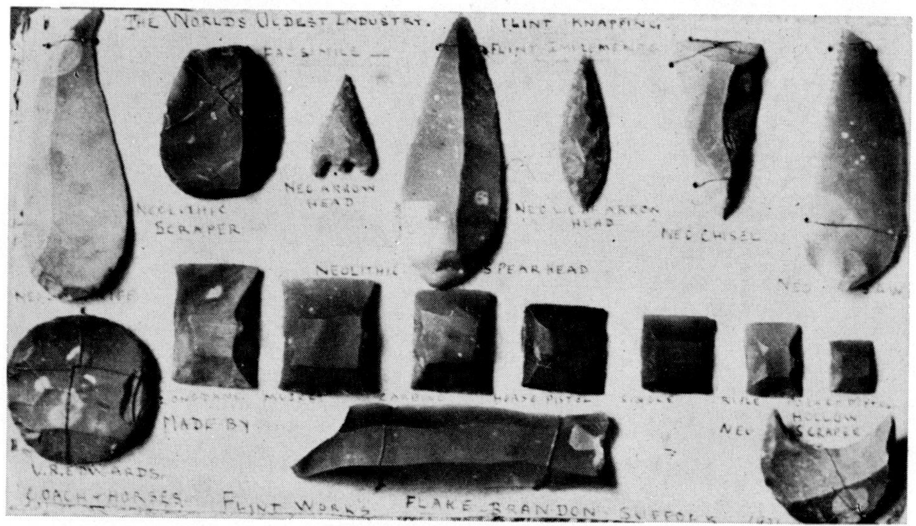

Stone Age Replicas made by Vic Edwards 1921

Stone Age flint mining implements

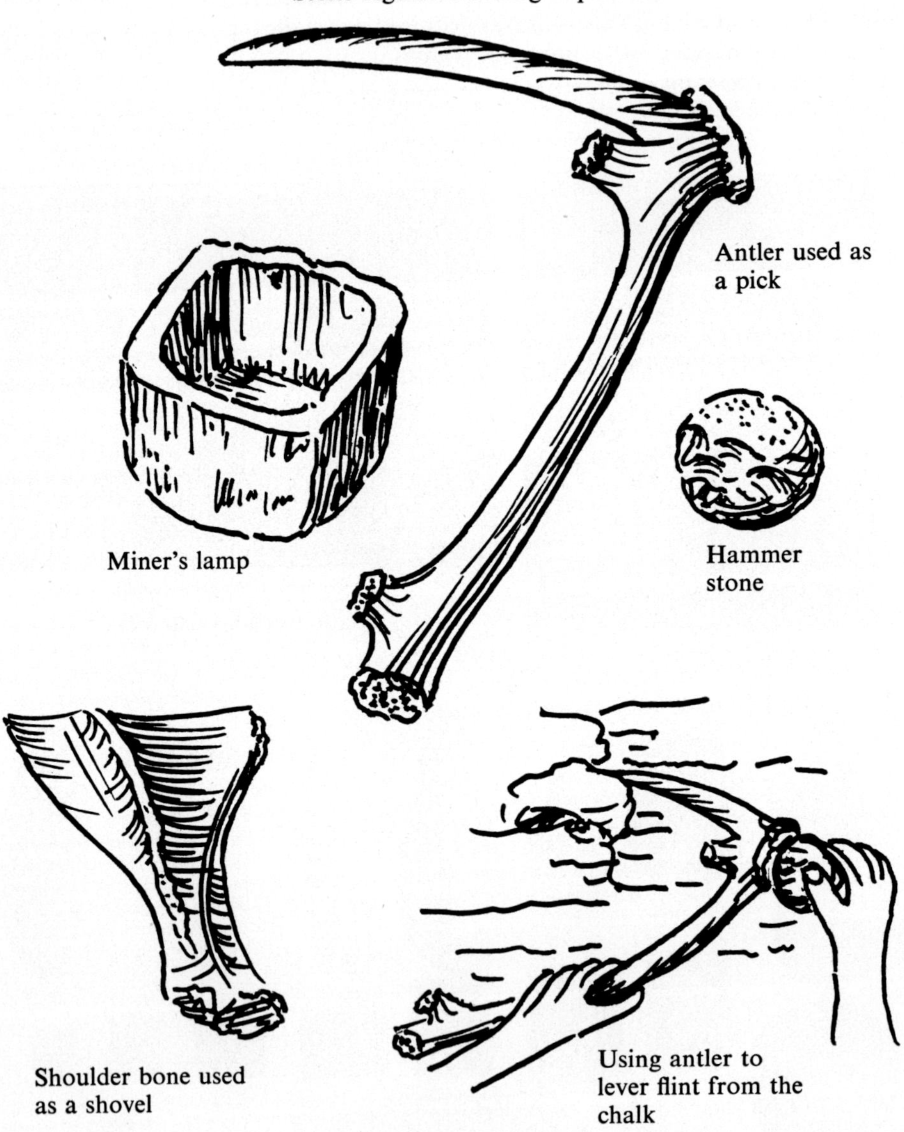

In searching for flints, Neolithic man discovered that large quantities could be mined from the chalk, particularly in parts of Sussex and at the site now known as 'Grimes Graves' near Brandon in Suffolk. Flints were mined by digging a large hole down to the floorstone and then tunnelling into the flint layers. At Blackpatch in Sussex, a mine which was investigated had a diameter of 17 feet and a depth of 10 feet. The walls were vertical—or nearly so—and had openings into seven galleries. One gallery had broken through into another gallery leading into another shaft. The average height of the galleries was $2\frac{1}{2}$ feet and the maximum height never exceeded 3 feet. The galleries varied in length from 5 feet to 30 feet and were from 3 to 6 feet wide.

It was found that firmly embedded nodules of flint had not always been extracted, which is not surprising in view of the primitive tools which the miners possessed. For picks they used deer antlers, which could be sharpened and then driven into the chalk. They were just the right shape for levering out the chalk or flints. For shovels they used shoulder blades from which the spine had been trimmed to give the maximum amount of flat area.

Canon Greenwell demonstrated that similar mines existed at Grimes Graves. He started excavating one of the numerous hollows on the site in 1868 and took three years to show that the depression was, in fact, the infilled shaft of a mine. Since then, more of the shafts have been opened and investigations made. Some have been kept open and are available to the public. The site is approached from the B1108, between Brandon and Thetford.

The arrival in Britain of warrior invaders known as the 'Beaker Folk' heralded the start of the first Bronze Age in about 1900 B.C. Although these people had some knowledge of metal they still used flint flakes for tipping their arrows, flint axes and other flint tools. They had also discovered how to make pottery which was a skill unknown to the natives.

The pottery was decorated either with a cord or a square-toothed comb but was coarse in texture and not strong enough to withstand the direct heat of a fire. To cook their food, therefore, they resorted to a system of indirect heating. Flint nodules were heated in the fire and when they were hot enough were plunged into the pots containing water and other ingredients. Because the flints could withstand temperatures well above boiling point, it would have been possible to boil water and cook in this way.

However, the regular alternate heating and plunging into water eventually cracked the flint surface. Sometimes heaps several yards in diameter and a few feet thick, of cracked flints together with evidence of wood ash, can be found on sites where these 'pot boiler' folk lived.

2. THE NATURE AND ORIGIN OF FLINTS

Flints are composed almost entirely of silica but the exact way in which they were formed is still uncertain. It is thought that the silica may have been precipitated in a gelatinous form while the chalk, in which flints are found, was being formed. Some geologists, however, consider that it may have been formed from percolating ground water during the Tertiary era which followed the Cretaceous period during which chalk was deposited. The silica may have been derived from the skeletons of sponges which are occasionally found as the nuclei of flint nodules.

When freshly broken, flint has a translucent appearance, varying from shades of grey to black. Each nodule or stone has an outer layer which is called the cortex, patina or 'coat'. This varies in thickness and colour, depending on how long the stone has been in its particular surroundings. A flint dug from chalk has a white patina but after it has been exposed for a number of years it may absorb other chemicals such as iron oxides from the soil and thus change colour. A flint on a beach, subjected to continuous wave action will have little or no patina.

Flints are the most common stones found in a large part of England south of a line from the river Tees to the Bristol Channel, excluding the south-western counties. In some places they are found in close proximity to chalk but elsewhere they occur in soils from which the chalk has been eroded or to which they were brought by glaciers during the Ice Ages. Large deposits of small flint stones or gravel are found mainly in estuarine areas. Many beaches are made of pebbles, most of which are of flint origin. Sometimes these have been carried by longshore drift to form extensive spits, a good example being Chesil Bill.

The story of flint begins in the late part of the Secondary or Mesozoic era. Fossil records show that the earth had already been in existence for many hundreds of millions of years before this era began. Already large mountain ranges consisting of Carboniferous, Silurian, Cambrian and other ancient rocks had been thrown up during periods of convulsive movements of the earth's crust.

The Secondary era lasted for about 120 million years. During the last 35-40 million years of this, huge chalk deposits of the Cretaceous period were formed. In this period, which ended about 65 million years ago, up to 80 per cent of the surface of the earth was flooded and large land living animals such as the Dinosaurus became extinct.

The vast ocean which covered most of the British Isles contained astronomical numbers of small and large shell fish. Indications are that the climate was warm, and this, combined with the moderate depth of water, was ideal for these marine creatures. After they died their disintegrating shells formed a chalky ooze which eventually became compressed into a comparatively dry rock. In this way chalk was built up at the rate of about one foot every thirty thousand years.

On the basis of its nature and composition, the Cretaceous chalk is divided into three main divisions: the lower, middle and upper. Further sub-divisions are made according to the different fossil species which are found in them.

The lower division contains a layer of chalk marl, which is used for manufacturing cement, but silica is dispersed and not aggregated into flints.

At its upper limit the middle chalk is marked by a layer of chalk rock, below which are found the flints which form the 'floorstone' of the Neolithic miners, and later, the miners of the Brandon area of Suffolk. These flints are found in a distinct layer and are therefore described as tabular.

Flints are found throughout the upper chalk. Sometimes these are tabular and sometimes scattered as nodules. The upper chalk varies considerably in thickness as it has been more affected by erosion than the lower layers. In some parts of the south of England it has been eroded completely but in others (Norfolk and the Isle of Wight), all the sub-divisions are still present.

'Floorstone' at the bottom of one of the pits
at Grimes Graves

3. FLINT MINING AND KNAPPING

In historical times, flint-knapping reached a peak of activity in the period of the Napoleonic Wars, when large numbers of gun-flints were used by the British Army. During the last quarter of the 18th century knappers could be found anywhere where there was a good supply of flints.

Sometimes a chalk or gravel quarry would yield only enough flints to keep one knapper at work but at Clarenden, near Salisbury, there were enough to supply a number of knappers, who worked on the edge of the road near the quarry. At Beer Head in Devon, where veins of flints can still be seen in the cliffs, knapping must have been a rather intermittent occupation, for knappers depended on cliff falls for their flints.

Flint Knapping—Town sign at Brandon, Suffolk

Another centre of activity was on the Thames, near Grays, where a good supply of flints from extensive chalk quarries kept a number of knappers fully occupied. But it was in the Suffolk town of Brandon where gun-flint manufacture had its stronghold and it is here, among the flint-built cottages, that flint knapping still continues.

There is little doubt that many of the knappers working in other parts of the country during the boom period, learnt their craft at Brandon and many only left the area temporarily to use flints where they were available in other areas.

The greatest migration occurred in the early years of the 19th century, when some of the Brandon men left their homes to work at nearby Icklingham when a good supply of best quality flint was found.

In 1686 a Government factory was established in Brandon and during the time that flintlock guns were used, all the Army's requirements were made there.

Brandon gun-flints became recognised for their outstanding quality because of the nature of the floorstone from which they were knapped. It was the same vein of flint which Neolithic man had mined, that brought fame to the town. Perhaps the floorstone was at first obtained from quarries dug into the chalk, in order to supply raw materials for the whiting industry but later it was mined on a large area of barren Breckland known as Lingheath.

When parts of the parish were enclosed by Act of Parliament in 1807, special provision was made for Lingheath. It was stated that '116 acres of steril land were awarded in trust that the rents and profits thereof should be laid out in purchasing fuel for distribution among the poor parishioners.' In 1826 the whole area was let for an annual rent of £16 but the trustees retained the right to take flints from a quarry 'which is let at a groundage rent of five shillings for every load of flints taken from it.' Some idea of the activity can be gained from the accumulation of £750 during the Napoleonic Wars.

Later, when flint was mined rather than quarried, the groundage rent was nearer one shilling per load but this depended on the value of the flint. Care was taken by the trustees to ensure that each miner had his fair share of the available land.

Miners, who usually worked singly, could have a pit which was being actively worked and a set of marks where it was intended to dig the next shaft. The marks were merely pieces of chalk or sods dug from the ground and could only be placed in position by permission of the trustees. It was their job to ensure that a new shaft would be far enough away from any other shaft to ensure that a good supply of flints could be obtained.

Eventually, Lingheath was covered with small pits where shafts had been dug but the land has now been levelled off.

The miners did not have to pay groundage or royalty but the knappers did. In 1876, Skertchley recorded the following costs per 'jag' or cartload to the knappers, of the various grades of flint from Lingheath.

	Floorstone		*Wall stone*		*Toppings*		*Upper Crust*	
Stone	6s.	6d.	5s.	0d.	3s.	6d.	3s.	6d.
Groundage	1s.	8d.		10d.		10d.		10d.
Cartage	1s.	0d.	1s.	0d.	1s.	0d.	1s.	0d.
Total	9s.	2d.	6s.	10d.	5s.	4d.	5s.	4d.

A 'jag' of ordinary quality stone would make 6,000 gun-flints, while good quality would give 12,000 and the best, 18,000. In addition, some of the cores could be dressed and sold for building. Large pieces of waste were suitable for roads and small chips for garden paths. Thousands of tons of waste were used in building the Great Eastern railway track through the area.

When mining on Lingheath, a start was made by digging the sand and gravel at the top, making a hole 10 feet by 3 feet, with a depth of up to 10 feet. This was usually sufficient to reach the chalk and as this was firmer it was possible to dig the next stage of the shaft from 5 to 6 feet deep and only just wide enough for the miner to drop down and climb up again when carrying pieces of flint. Each stage was orientated at right angles to the one above and had toe holes cut into the sides forming a staircase up which the miner could climb. The pits were dug with a series of ledges so that when the bottom was reached it was 10 to 12 feet away from the perpendicular line of the opening. Sometimes the pits were 40 feet deep before the most precious layer of floorstone was reached.

The first stage was aligned to admit the maximum amount of sunlight but as the mine became deeper insufficient light came down the shaft so that for light the miner had to rely on a candle attached to his cap. The candle also served as a timepiece, as by knowing how long it took to burn down he could estimate the passing of time.

On Lingheath there were three layers of flint, each of which was mined by cutting galleries into the chalk.

The first layer, which was about 15 feet from the surface, was the 'topstone' or toppings. This was a more or less continuous layer of what the miners called 'hobbly' stones because they had 'paps' or knobs on their upper sides. These flints did not flake cleanly, were coarse working, and since good gun-flints could not be made from them were mainly used for building.

Below the toppings was a layer of hard chalk which contained scattered flints called the upper crust. These were not of high quality but were extracted while the shaft was being dug.

The second layer was about 25 feet from the surface. These flints also had 'paps' on their upper surface but in addition, had horn-like projections below. Sometimes the horns were up to 2 inches long and as they were embedded in the chalk they made removal of this layer very difficult. These flints, known as 'wallstone' generally gave a black knapped surface but sometimes it was grey or spotted. As they were a better quality than the toppings and flaked well, they could be knapped into gun-flints or 'builders'.

The third and last layer of flint was the 'floorstone'. It consisted of large pieces of stone varying from a few inches to several yards across, with rounded or ovoid knobs and generally about 6 inches thick. 'Floorstone' flaked cleanly, giving a uniform black surface of fine and even texture. From it the best quality 'Brandon Black' flints were made. It was this same flint that Neolithic man sought in the mines at Grimes Graves.

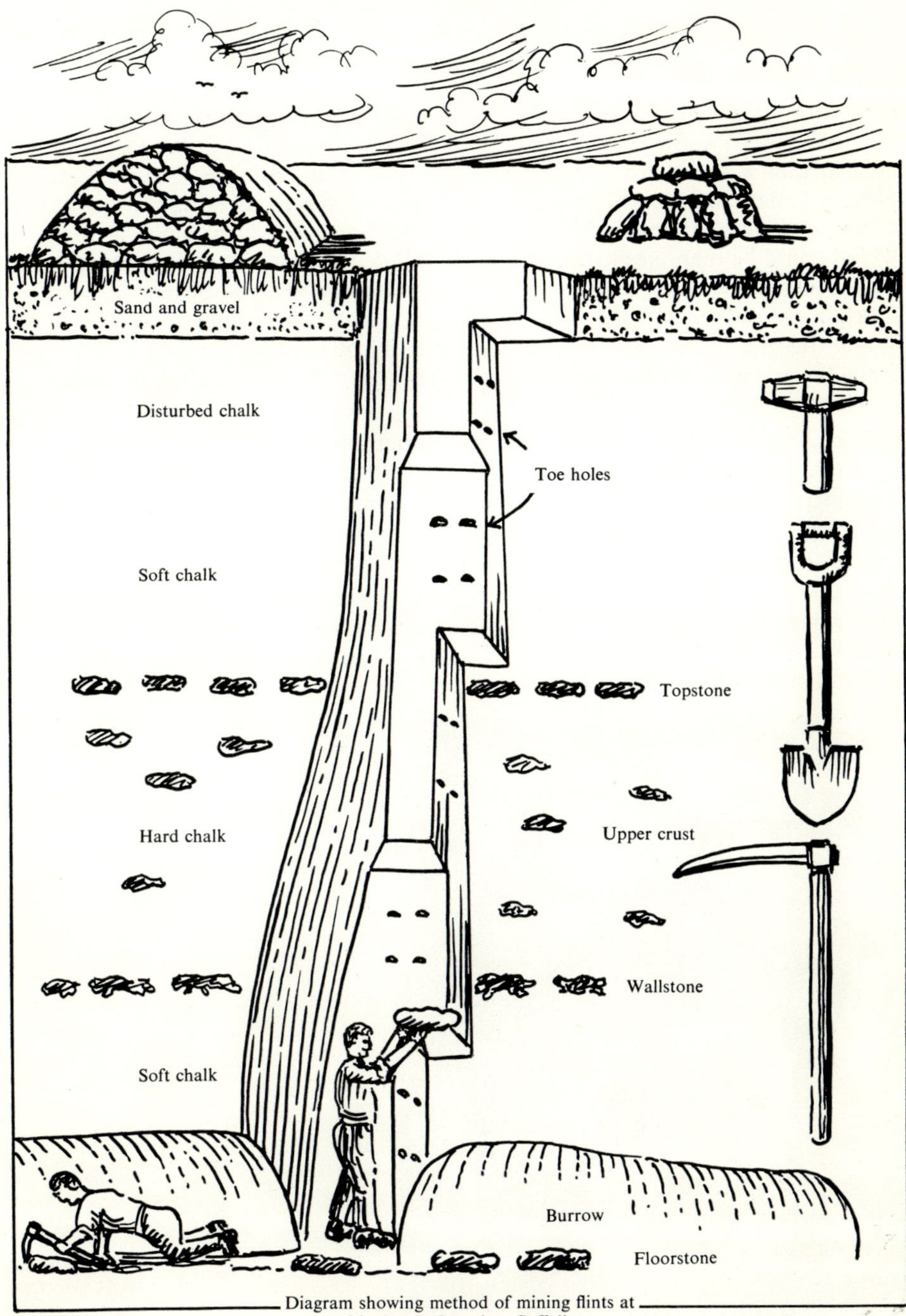

Diagram showing method of mining flints at Lingheath, Brandon, Suffolk

In sinking a shaft, a miner removed as little as possible of the chalk and flints but as soon as the floorstone had been reached, tunnelling for it was commenced. The miner used three tools for most of his work—a spade for removing sand and chalk, a pick (similar in shape to the antler horns used by Neolithic man) and a heavy hammer weighing from 5 to 7 lb. Occasionally he also used a short crowbar to heave a lump of flint from the chalk. Using the pick, a gallery was made into the chalk so that pieces of floorstone could be removed. The heavy hammer was needed to break the large slabs into pieces which could be manhandled up the shaft. While the first gallery was being made all the chalk had also to be carried to the surface. To minimise the work as much as possible, galleries were made only just big enough to crawl along. When the first gallery was worked out it could be used for depositing the spoil from the second gallery thus making subsequent working of the mine a little less laborious.

To get the slabs to the surface the miner lifted pieces from one stage to another, eventually reaching the surface. Sometimes the miners helped each other with this part of the operation when there would be a man standing at each stage to form a human chain from top to bottom.

After all the floorstone had been taken out, the wallstone was worked in the same way and after it was worked out the topstone was mined. A shaft took about three weeks to dig, and to remove the flints took from six to nine months. Miners were paid one shilling by the trustees for filling in the shaft after all the flints had been removed.

'Pony' Ashley —at second stage

The last miner on Lingheath was 'Pony' Ashley, who worked until he was over 80. Since he stopped work in the late 1930's, flints have been obtained from nearby chalk pits. One person, Anne Peacock, who remembered 'Pony' described him as she was accustomed to seeing him 'walking home from Lingheath with a sack on his back and white from top to toe with chalk from the flint pits. As a small girl I wanted to see what the flint pits were like so I walked up to the heath and waited for Pony to come up from his pit. As he was a quiet man I suppose he was quite surprised to see a small girl of about eleven waiting for him. He was very kind and patiently told me about the pits and the way he had worked there all his life. It was a hard life, both in digging the shaft and in lifting the huge heavy slabs of flint to the surface. He lived a very lonely life. I shall never forget the beautiful stillness and quietness of Lingheath and the days which I spent there with this grand old man.'

It was the flint knappers' work to dress flints into gun-flints or into shapes and sizes which builders could use. Knappers preferred to use freshly dug flint as it was easier to work and flaked more predictably. To keep it in the best possible condition it was sprinkled with water to prevent it from becoming too dry in the summer, and if it had become too wet during periods of prolonged rain, it was put round the fire to dry it slightly.

Making gun-flints involved the three separate operations of quartering, flaking and knapping.

For quartering the knapper wore a leather pad on his left knee, as well as a leather apron. The nodule of flint, varying in weight from a few pounds to a half cwt was placed on the knee pad. For quartering, an iron hammer with a hexagonal head which was only slightly tapered to give it a large face, was used. The largest quartering hammers weighed about seven lb and the smallest about three lb, and were used according to the size of the nodule.

When the knapper tapped the nodule he was able to tell from the sound which way he could best break it into pieces suitable for flaking. No force was needed and all that was necessary was for the hammer to fall onto the nodule to sever it along a line of cleavage. The object was to produce a square edge from which flakes could be struck. The pieces usually had faces about six inches square.

The second process, flaking, required great skill to produce flakes of the size needed. A hammer with a small face of a half-inch square was used. The quarter had to be struck at the proper angle, at the exact spot, with the minimum of force needed to dislodge the flake. Flakes were struck off until only a small core was left. The first ones were up to six inches long but later ones were progressively shorter, depending on the shape of the quarter. A skilled flaker could produce 5,000 to 7,000 flakes per day.

Thetford: The Ancient House Museum

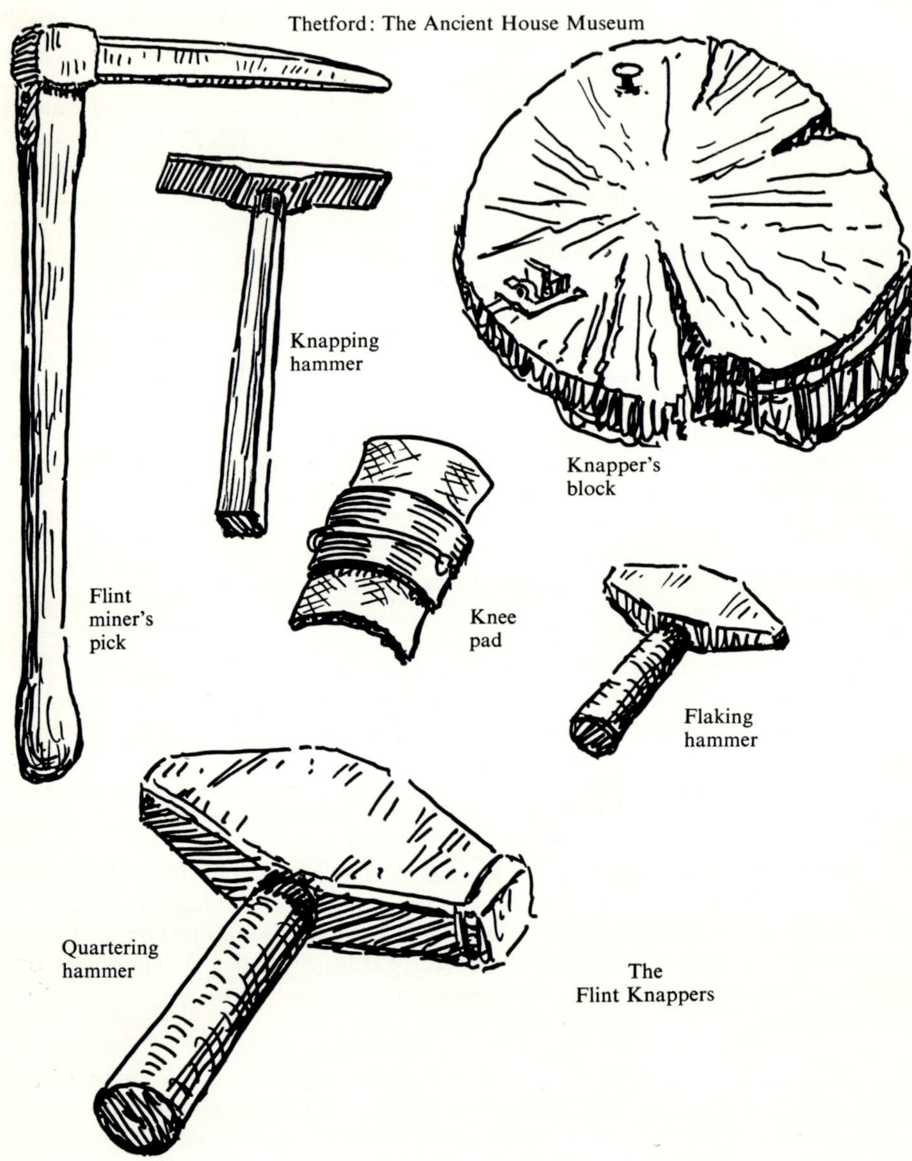

The Flint Knappers

The third, and last, operation was to knap the flakes into gun-flints. The hammer used for this was made from an old steel file, nine inches long, one inch wide and a quarter-inch thick. The edge had to be kept square by filing and tempering it regularly.

For knapping, the worker sat at a block made from the stump of an oak tree. Into the block was set a small anvil against which the flakes were held. It was surrounded by a leather pad which gave resilience when the knapper's hammer was tapped rhythmically as the flake was turned round, ready for the next tap. Three edges of the flake were trimmed as it was turned in an anti-clockwise direction, and the fourth side of the gun-flint was cut as it was struck off the flake.

Flaking

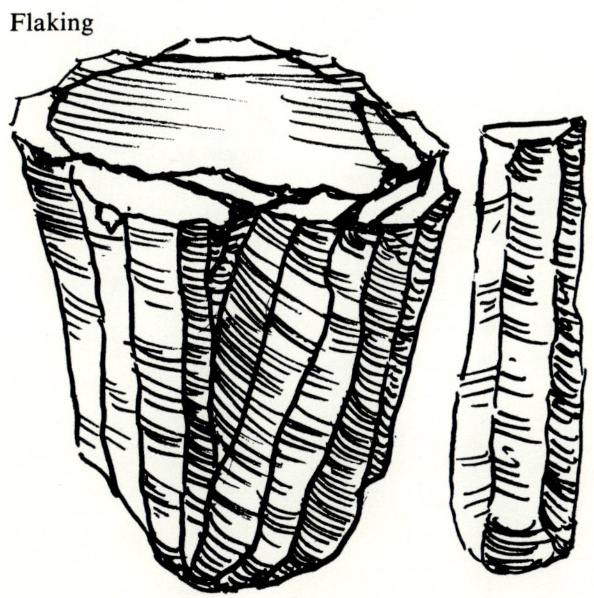

Flint nodule showing system of flaking

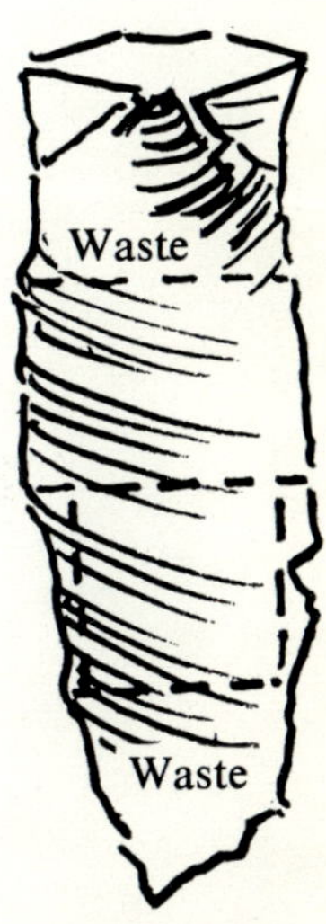

Flake, showing how two flints could be knapped from it

Photo] [*Hallam Ashley*

H. Field—quartering

Photo] [*Hallam Ashley*

H. Field—flaking

Photo] [*Hallam Ashley*

H. Field—knapping

Experienced knappers judged the size of the flints which they made by eye and when finished would cast them into separate tins according to size as appropriate. The largest flints were used in muskets, smaller ones in carbines or rifles and the smallest in pistols. An experienced knapper could produce up to 300 flints per hour providing he had good flakes on which to work.

Before selling, all the gun-flints had to be counted. The tin was emptied onto a table or bench and the flints counted by drawing three with the right hand and two with the left. The group of five, known as a 'cast', was drawn aside or placed straight into a receptacle. Knappers have been known to count 20,000 in an hour using this method.

The cores from which flakes had been knapped were worked slightly so that they could be used by builders. Sometimes they were squared to a definite size, and sometimes were rounded, depending on what was needed at the time. Inferior flints which were not suitable for gun-flints were also knapped for buildings. The best quality were either square or round 'black-faced' and the inferior grades were classified as 'mixed-coloured'. These latter flints would vary in colour from a very pale grey to nearly black according to the source of the stone from which they were knapped.

Flints which were not big enough for knapping into top quality 'builders' were sold as 'random faced'. They were of any size or colour but could be used for flushwork as they had a face which had been exposed by knapping.

A lower quality was obtained from the irregular pieces broken off during quartering. These were known as 'rough builders' and were much cheaper for the builders to buy but could not be used to give a very good finish to a wall. Builders also used land stones which were picked from fields or beaches and not dressed at all.

Knappers often worked in sheds in their own gardens. Their employer would collect the gun-flints once a week and at the same time bring a supply of freshly mined flints for use during the next week. Sometimes two or three knappers worked together if a building of some sort was available. During the cold weather they often worked in a confined space with inadequate heating. To eliminate the draughts from windows and doors any gaps were blocked with hessian sacking.

As there was no ventilation, the miners worked under the worst possible conditions in an atmosphere made hazy with the dust from their busy hammers and they were continuously inhaling this fine dust, which caused silicosis and the premature death of many a knapper.

This danger was overcome by installing an electric dust extractor. It had a three inch diameter pipe leading down to, and over, the working area which took the dust to an outlet in the workshop wall.

4. FLINT GLASS

Glass is made from silica (sand), soda and other minor ingredients which are fused together at very high temperatures. The molten glass is poured into moulds or 'blown' into the required shape. After it has cooled it is finished by polishing, engraving or cutting.

Very little glass was made in this country until the beginning of the 17th century. This may have been partly due to the lack of suitable fuel other than wood. A writer in 1577 declared that,

> 'As for glass makers they be scant in this land,
> Yet one there is as I do understand
> And in Sussex is now his habitation
> At Chiddingsfold he works at his occupation.'

A patent for a furnace which burnt coal during the manufacture of glass was purchased by Sir Robert Mansell in 1615. The government, anxious to check the consumption of wood for industrial purposes, immediately prohibited the manufacture of glass with wood and at the same time, banned the importation of glass. This encouraged foreign glass makers to come to this country and establish their glass works here.

By the middle of the 17th century a number of Italian glass makers, famous for their Venetian glass, were working in and around London. For almost a century in their native country, flint had been used as the main source of silica for glass making. This was derived from flint pebbles obtained from the bed of the river Ticino. The pebbles were first heated to a high temperature and then broken and ground into a fine powder which could be used instead of sand. Some of the Italians continued to use their traditional source of flints but they had to turn to local supplies when imported pebbles were not available.

When the ban on importing glass was lifted, George Ravenscroft, a London merchant, found difficulty in meeting an ever increasing demand for the very fine Venetian glass. The shortage was caused to some extent by the fragile nature of flint glass. Even while standing on a shelf, vessels would suddenly crack and disintegrate. In transit on ships and by pack-horses, breakages were so high that it became customary to send 25 per cent more than was ordered in the hope that enough would arrive unbroken to fulfil the order.

Ravenscroft decided that he would make his own glass and in 1673, when he erected his first small glass house, he used flint and Spanish potash. Unfortunately, the glass which he made gradually lost its transparency and was not, therefore, a satisfactory substitute for Venetian crystal.

To overcome this defect he tried the effects of adding new ingredients to his raw materials. Eventually he discovered that the addition of a small amount of lead oxide would produce a glass with a refractive brilliance superior to any other which was being made at that time. His new glass was at first called 'improved flint glass', then 'English crystal' and ultimately 'lead crystal'.

Flint continued to be used for some years and in 1696 there were still 27 flint glass houses operating in this country. It is by no means certain that they were all still using flint instead of sand. The use of flint was made easier by the invention, in 1691, of a mill by John Tyzache. After having been heated, the flints were crushed into a powder by mixing them with stones and rolling them round a trough with a marble base. The crushed flint was sifted through a buckram bag. To limit the amount of dust, sifting was done in a closed bin. Two sleeves permitted the workmen to shake the bag about without creating dust.

In spite of the improvements made in the preparation of crushed flint, its use soon declined. Ravenscroft's process of using lead oxide with sand gradually grew in popularity. After the early years of the 18th century flint was no longer used but the term 'flint glass' has remained and because of the continuing use of this term it is difficult to distinguish when flint has actually been used in the manufacturing process. It has been said, for instance, that although Stourbridge flint glass became world famous it is very doubtful whether any flints were ever used in its making.

Long Melford Church, Suffolk

5. THE USE OF FLINTS IN POTTERY

Large quantities of calcined flints are used in the manufacture of a wide range of pottery, including table and sanitary ware, glazes and tiles. It was first included in the 'body' of the potter's clay as a whitening agent but other benefits were discovered from its use. The 'body' was stiffened, easier to work and flat articles such as tiles did not warp.

A Staffordshire potter named John Astbury is first thought to have used flints about 1720. The process became very popular and by the time Queen Victoria came to the throne it was estimated that about 800,000 tons of flints were being used annually in the potteries.

Most of the flints now come from chalk pits in the south of England or are imported from Normandy and Belgium. Pebble-strewn beaches of south and east England, together with the beaches of Normandy, were the original sources of flints.

In the early 18th century flints were carried in small smacks and barges along the rivers Trent, Severn, Dee and Mersey and unloaded at quays as near to the potteries as possible. As roads were very poor and were impassable by horses and carts during adverse weather, pack-horses were frequently the only means of transporting the flints from the quays. Long strings of horses were employed in this way. On their return journey they carried pottery back to markets or to the barges.

The prodigious quantities of materials which had to be carried added greatly to the potter's costs. A cheaper method of transport was sought by Josiah Wedgwood who, by the middle of the century, had a thriving and expanding business. He sought the help of James Brindley to construct the Trent and Mersey Canal which was authorised by Act of Parliament in 1766. In July of that year Wedgwood dug the first sod and by 1772 the first hundred miles had been completed. This was the section from the Trent to the potteries. It took another five years to join up with the Mersey, mainly because of engineering difficulties in cutting the Harecastle tunnel. The canal, which is estimated to have cost £300,000, gave regular, reliable and cheaper means of transporting raw materials and products to and from the potteries.

After completion of the canal Runcorn became the main port for flints and a considerable trade built up from the south coast and particularly Sussex. Using a big fleet of smacks, each about 30 feet long, fishermen and other seafarers became engaged in collecting 'boulders' from the shore. At high tide they grounded their craft on the pebbly beach, loading them at low tide so that they were ready to float off on the next high. At ports such as Rye and Newhaven the fishermen transhipped their 'boulders' into schooners, ketches and later, steam ships, for carrying to Runcorn. During the autumn when shoals of herrings were nearby, the fishermen reverted to using their smacks as drifters.

Collecting flints at Rye, Sussex in 1939

Photo] [*Dr. W. E. Snell*

A few men and women earned a living by picking flints into baskets and loading them into carts for delivery to the quay.

Limited quantities of flints are still obtained from beaches and in recent years up to 1,000 tons per year have been taken from the Seatown beach and large tonnages from near Dungeness.

The reason why flint was first used for pottery is open to conjecture but according to J. Wedgwood it started as a result of an accident to a potter's horse while on the way to London. The horse's eyes became inflamed and when the potter stopped at a hostelry, the innkeeper showed him how the animal's eyes could be treated. He roasted a flint until it became very brittle and cracked easily. The fragments were ground into a fine powder which was made into a poultice and applied to the horse's eyes. The potter was so impressed with the whiteness and fineness of the powder that he took some flints back with him on his return journey. He then experimented by adding the powder to his clay and found it improved his china.

It seems more probable, however, that the use of flint in pottery arose from its use in the manufacture of glass, as the preparation of flint powder was similar for both purposes.

1
2
3
4
5
6
7
8
9a
9c
10
11
12
13
14

One of the first mills for preparing flint in the potteries was built at Hanley in 1726 and another was constructed by James Brindley at Tunstall in 1757. Brindley's mill used a water wheel to drive the stampers which pounded the flints into powder. A year later he built another mill but this time it was driven by wind power. He went on to build a number of mills, including one at Cheddleton, near Leek, which has been restored and opened to the public by the Cheddleton Flint Mill Industrial Heritage Trust.

The processing of flint at Cheddleton is shown diagrammatically on page 30.

(1) Caldon canal completed in 1777.

(2) Narrow boats brought stones, flints and coal and returned with the ground flint to the potteries. Flints came from Runcorn via the river Weaver and the Trent and Mersey Canal.

(3) The crane was used to unload heavy stones to be used as parers and runners.

(4) Parers were chert stones used to pave the floor of the grinding pans.

(5) Runners were also chert with heavier veins of limestone, and softer than the parers.

(6) Flint kilns for calcining the flints. The kilns were loaded with alternate layers of coal and flint and burnt for about three days. One hundredweight of coal was used with one ton of flints. Heating drove off water and cracked the flints. A temperature of 450°C was needed to complete the dehydration but it frequently rose to 900°C.

(7) Calcined flints were drawn off and taken to the mill.

(8) Plateway and waggon.

(9) Auxiliary shafting driven by the vertical shaft of the pan drive, the hoist (9a) which raised the flints to the first floor, the water pump and the slip pump (9c) which pumped the ground material from the settling ark to the drying kiln.

(10) The pan would hold about $1\frac{1}{2}$ tons of calcined flints and would grind for 24 hours. Then the thick creamy fluid was run off into the wash tub.

(11) In the wash tub the flint was mixed with a large volume of water and thoroughly mixed and dispersed by rotating the wooden gates. This separated the fine and coarse particles. The fine particles were discharged into the settling ark (12) while the coarse were returned to the pan.

(13) The plug plank. When the flint had settled clear water was drawn off by removing the plugs progressively until flint itself appeared. The remainder was then pumped into the slip drying kiln (14). After all the water had been evaporated, the flint was removed in blocks for despatch to the potteries.

Today, flints are heated in continuous kilns which can be recharged with coal and flints, the resulting calcined flints and ash being taken from the bottom. Kilns using gas fuel are also used. Grinding is done in ball mills which contain beach pebbles as iron balls cause staining in the flint powder. This process is still carried out in water to avoid the creation of dust.

Water wheel, Cheddleton Flint Mill,
Leek, Staffordshire

6. BUILDINGS AND ROADS

Throughout much of the eastern and southern counties of England, from Norfolk to Dorset, flint is the most common naturally occurring stone suitable for building. In these areas a cottage, church, wall, bridge or some other type of building constructed at least in part with flint can be found in almost every town or village. In some localities as, for example, the Brecklands of Norfolk and Suffolk or on some parts of coastal stretches in Norfolk and Sussex, flint is the principal building material in all the older streets.

Flints were used extensively by the Romans in those parts of the country where there was an abundant supply which could easily be picked up from fields and beaches. The hardness and durability of the flints made them ideal for fortifications such as castles and city walls.

Constructing strong walls from irregular and often rounded flints called for considerable skill. As the flints fitted loosely together large quantities of mortar were needed to fill the spaces and therefore a supply of chalk was essential. On the exterior of walls made in this way there is sometimes more mortar to be seen than flints. Construction was very slow as after a little had been done it had to be left for the mortar to harden before any more was put above it. If this was not done, there was every likelihood of the flints slipping from the mortar, causing the wall to collapse.

Flint packhorse bridge, Moulton, Suffolk

Some idea of the quantity of flints used can be gained from examining the remains of some of the Roman walls. At Burgh Castle, overlooking the river Waveney in Suffolk, some walls are 15 feet high, with a width of 11 feet at the bottom and 6 feet at the top.

In some Roman walls flint rubble formed the centre, while the face was of stone or brick but now, in many cases, only the flint part remains. When it has been necessary to break into these walls it has been found that after nearly 2,000 years, the mortar can be more difficult to break than the flints themselves.

A feature of many of the early flint forts and castles is the absence of square corners. At Pevensey, for example, the great wall which encloses about 10 acres is ovoid and the individual forts are all semi-circular. This is because it is extremely difficult to make satisfactory corners with natural unknapped flints.

Flushwork, Long Melford Church, Suffolk

A large number of the parish churches in Norfolk and Suffolk, which are built mainly of flint, have round towers for this same reason. The towers were built in the 11th and 12th centuries and were probably first used as look-outs, being incorporated into the parish churches later.

During the Middle Ages flint was used in an unknapped state but it was not unusual for the builders to select stones of even size for the exterior so that a semblance of courses can be seen. For the corners or quoins, it became customary to use a single row of stones or bricks. Caen and Barnack stone were very popular for this purpose.

Flint Church, South Acre, Norfolk

Cromer Church, Norfolk

In the 15th century flint flushwork began to be used. The flint nodules were knapped to expose a flat surface and were squared so that they could be fitted together, in the same way as bricks. Because of the accuracy of the knapping only a small band of mortar was necessary to hold them together. Knapping for building developed into a fine craft. Pieces of flint were produced to fit into elaborate designs outlined in stonework.

Very fine examples of flushwork can be seen in Essex on the 15th century gatehouse of St. Osyth Priory and of St. John's Abbey, Colchester. One of the finest flushwork church towers in the country, at Redenhall, near Harleston in Norfolk was built between 1460 and 1520.

Sometimes squares of flushwork and stone were used alternately to give a chequered appearance, as at the Guildhalls at King's Lynn and Norwich and the Marlipins, near Shoreham in Sussex.

Flushwork was used to decorate buttresses but there is often more stone work than flint.

As large amounts of mortar were exposed because the natural flints could not be fitted closely together, small stones or flint flakes were sometimes stuck in the mortar to protect it from the weather and for decoration. This practice is known variously as 'garetting', 'galleting' or 'garneting'. On some buildings in north-west Norfolk small pebbles of reddish brown carstone have been used for this purpose.

Galleting with flint flakes
The Guildhall
Norwich, Norfolk

Flint and brick wall with
galleting of carstone pebbles
Shouldham, Norfolk

Flints are still used for building in some areas where an exterior wall is required to blend with other older walls in a village or town, but only the facing is of flint. If unknapped flints are used they are graded to a certain size so that they can be built in courses. Knapped flints have been used in recent years on bungalows built at Castle Acre by the Norfolk County Council.

On some modern buildings precast flint panels have been used. Sometimes they are made of knapped flints but in some cases a mixture of whole and knapped flints is used, giving an appearance which resembles older flintwork although the individual flints used in the modern work are much smaller.

Precast flint panels, Thetford, Norfolk

In those parts of the country where they could be easily obtained, flints formed the base material for roads for many centuries. The Romans used hard compacted chalk as a foundation for their roads and this was covered with a layer of large flints when available. Finally, gravel was spread over the surface to make it smooth enough for men and horses to walk along.

Until 1888, when the Local Government Act was passed, road repairs were the responsibility of the parish councils. In parts of East Anglia flints were the only locally available raw material and these could be picked from cultivated fields. In fact, the extremely large number of flints on the ground caused such excessive wear and tear to farmers' ploughs and cultivating implements that they were glad to have them picked off their fields. Stone-picking was used as a means of giving employment to out-of-work men who qualified for parish relief. Usually it was the women and children who did the picking in late winter and early spring when the stones were clearly exposed and before treading damaged the young crop. It was very unpopular work on account of its monotonous, tedious and arduous nature. However, the near destitute poor were anxious to earn some money even if they were only paid a penny for each bucket of stones.

After the district and county councils had taken over responsibility for road maintenance a demand for large supplies of flints developed. In the early 1890's Essex County Council obtained flints from Kentish chalk quarries for use in coastal areas. They were transported by water to various places where they were off-loaded at one of the numerous quays in the rivers and creeks, or onto carts after the barge had been beached. At one time 20 barges from Faversham were engaged almost entirely on this work.

Large rounded stones called cobbles were at one time popular for use on streets in towns. Any round stone of suitable size is called a cobble and the name is not used exclusively for flints. Most of the cobbled streets in the south-east are composed almost entirely of cobbles which have been taken from

West Stow Church, Suffolk

Norwich Guildhall, Norfolk

beaches where constant pounding by the waves gradually eroded them to the required shape and size. Cobbles set into concrete are still used for paving small areas of pedestrian precincts and for decorative display round trees, seats and many other objects. Small rounded flints are used for pathways, or as an edging to paved pathways, as in some of the college quadrangles at Cambridge.

By far the greatest amount of flint used in buildings and roads is in the form of small pebbles or gravel, which is the aggregate used in making concrete.

Crushed calcined flint, which is graded into 10 different sizes, is used in building and for roads. It can be used as an aggregate with white cement to produce concrete, which is especially strong and permanently white. It is also incorporated into road surfaces to improve the light reflection and to increase tyre adhesion. Calcined flint mixed with white Portland cement is used for edge markings on motorways.

Random knapped flint wall
West Stow, Suffolk

Rounded flint pebble wall
Cromer, Norfolk

Chequer flintwork
The Guildhall, King's Lynn, Norfolk

Flushwork, Redenhall Church, Harleston, Norfolk

7. FLINTLOCK GUNS

Guns were first invented in the 14th century but they were of very limited use for warfare because of the difficulty of muzzle loading and their matchlock ignition. The 'match', which was really a smouldering piece of cord, was easily extinguished in wet or windy weather and the only method that the gunman had for relighting it was a flint strike-a-light.

To overcome this difficulty, spark ignition was developed. In 1517 the wheel lock was invented in Nuremburg. A piece of pyrites was held close to a metal wheel with serrated edges. After the gun had been loaded and primed, the wheel was turned by a strong spring, causing a shower of sparks which ignited the priming powder.

This ignition system suffered from two defects. Firstly, as the mechanism was complicated and difficult to make, the gun was expensive. Secondly, the pyrites was brittle and prone to break, so that its position had to be adjusted or a new piece of pyrites fixed before the gun could be fired.

It was realised that a more reliable source of sparks could be obtained from flint and steel, and, as a result, the flintlock gun was developed. The original 'snaphaunce' lock was not used very much in this country but some of the troops sent to Ireland in 1580 were probably armed with weapons with this type of flintlock.

During the first quarter of the 17th century the 'English' flintlock was invented. It was simpler, more reliable, and remained in use for over two centuries. The flint was held in the jaws of the cock. An L-shaped steel striking surface called the 'frizzen' was held in position covering the priming powder by a spring. When fired, the flint struck the frizzen, pushing it back and sending a shower of sparks towards the now exposed priming powder.

For safety, the cock could be held in a halfway position and the trigger could not then be operated. Sometimes accidents did occur and the gun was said to go off at 'half cock', hence the expression 'going off at half cock' which is still used when something is set in motion in an unprepared state.

It was during the Civil War, 1642 to 1651, that for the first time in the history of warfare, firearms were at least as important as other weapons in influencing the outcome of battles.

When Grenadier units were formed in 1671, the men were issued with flintlock carbines fitted with slings for carrying them on their shoulders. The gun was also known as a 'fuzil', after a light fowling piece imported from Italy. The name, which was derived from the Italian word for flint—'fucile'—was corrupted into 'fusiliers' by the troops armed with these weapons.

By about 1700 most of the matchlocks had been replaced by flintlocks.

A musket known as 'Brown Bess' was introduced in the early part of the 18th century and for over a century was the main hand weapon used by the

British Army. It was popular because it gave fewer misfires or 'flashes in the pan' than earlier guns. With this gun, muzzle loading was made easier as the troops were issued with special 'cartridges'. Each consisted of a tube of cartridge paper which contained 6 to 8 drachms of powder and a lead bullet. After biting off one end of the tube the soldier would shake a small portion of powder onto the flashpan and then empty the remainder down the barrel. The bullet was put down the barrel and held in position by using the cartridge paper as wadding and ramming it tight. Two or three rounds per minute could be loaded in this way.

The number of flintlocks used by the army reached a peak during the Napoleonic Wars, during which $3\frac{1}{2}$ million muskets alone were manufactured.

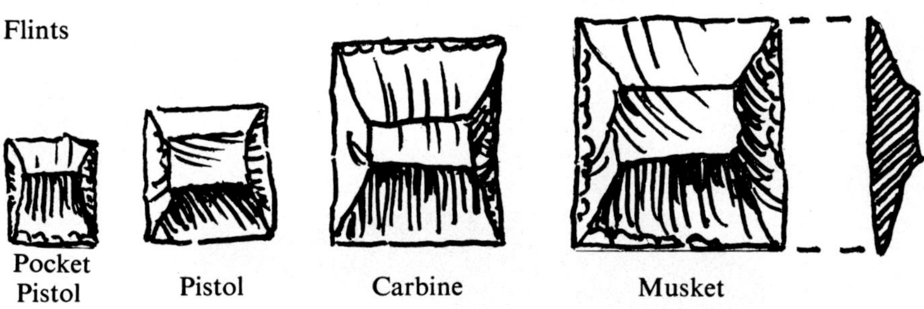

Flintlock pistols of many different sizes were also made, both for military and private use. The blunderbuss was another flintlock firearm, made primarily for personal protection. This gun had a barrel with an exceptionally wide bore and was designed to shoot a number of bullets at once. It was for use at close quarters and was a favourite weapon carried by stagecoach and mail van guards as a protection against highwaymen as it did not need to be aimed accurately.

Some of the most intricate work went into the production of fowling pieces and other sporting weapons. Famous makers of these guns include Joseph Manton, James Purdy and Henry Nock.

The production of a large number of flintlocks created an unprecedented demand for gun-flints. At first these were knapped from flints found at the surface in fields and waste land. This was not very satisfactory as the gun-flints were brittle and broke easily. As the stones were comparatively small, making gun-flints from them was tedious and very slow. By the middle of the 18th century, superior floorstone was being used and gun-flints of the highest known quality were being made.

The Development of the Flintlock

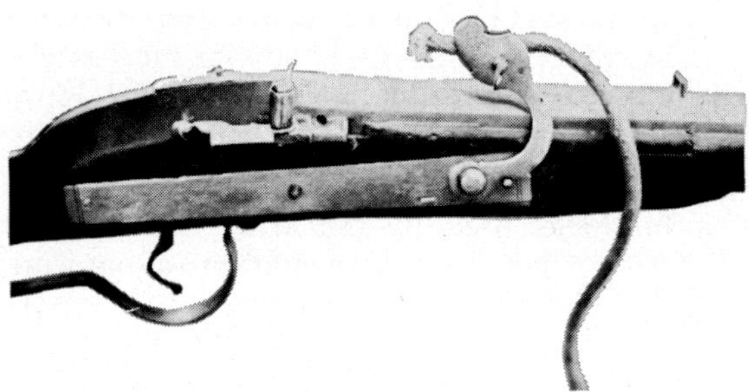

Matchlock musket of the type used by infantry in the Civil War

Wheel lock horseman's pistol (*about* 1580)

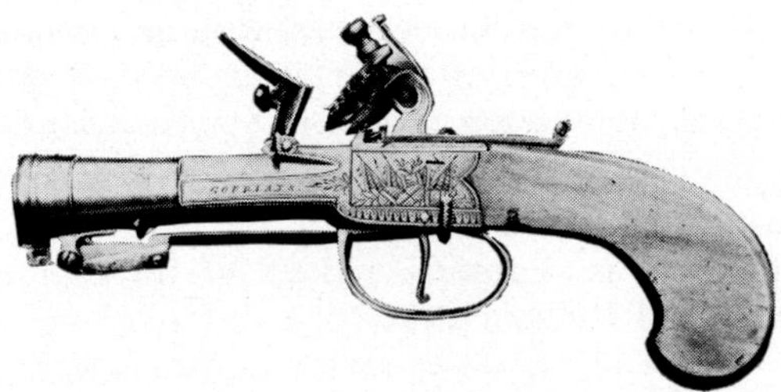

Flintlock pistol blunderbuss with folding spring bayonet (*about* 1790)

Photographs of firearms in the Glasgow Art Gallery and Museum
[*by courtesy of the Director*]

'Best' quality could be expected to give from 40 to 50 shots without fear of a misfire, whilst inferior 'common' flints would only give half this number.

Typical results of firing a flintlock pistol 100 times using best quality 'Brandon Black' flints were:

	First 25 *shots*	*Last* 25 *shots*	100 *shots*
Fired	20	2	34
Flashed only	1	—	7
Missed	4	23	59

As can be seen, the efficiency of the gun-flint gradually fell so that it had to be replaced from time to time. For this reason spare flints were carried in leather or cloth wallets.

In 1804, the British Army contracted with gun-flint makers in Brandon for the supply of 356,000 flints per month. These were to be supplied in the proportion of 50 carbine size and 50 pistol size for every 1,000 for muskets. The musket flints were priced at 21 shillings per 1,000. At this period, flints were packed and despatched in half-casks, which held 2,000 musket size, 3,000 carbine size and 4,000 pistol size.

At about this time a treaty with some of the Indian tribes in America established the value of 10 gun-flints as one deer skin. A gun was bartered for 16 deer skins, whilst for one deer skin either a pound of powder or 30 bullets could be obtained.

The heyday of the flintlock was soon to be over as in 1806 percussion ignition was invented by the Rev. Alexander John Forsyth. He was a keen wildfowler and was frequently exasperated that the interval between when the sparks struck the priming powder causing a flash and the ignition of the main charge, was sufficient for the wildfowl to take flight before the shot reached them. After some years of experimenting, he perfected his invention and took out a patent on it.

At first it was not adopted by the army but its value was soon realised by makers of sporting guns. In 1834 trials to compare flintlocks and percussion locks were carried out by the army at Woolwich. After 6,000 rounds had been fired the flintlocks had misfired 922 times, whereas the percussion locks had only missed 36 times. The superiority of the new invention was thus clearly demonstrated and within about 15 years the last of their flintlocks had been handed in by soldiers of the British Army.

This was by no means the end of flintlocks, many of which continued to be used by other armies. The disused weapons were sold in many parts of the world and in parts of Africa they were used until comparatively recently. They are still used in some countries for ceremonial occasions.

Muzzle-loading clubs, which use flintlock weapons, have a considerable following in Britain, parts of Europe and America.

8. STRIKE-A-LIGHTS AND STEEL MILLS

The art of creating fire was known to Stone Age man and among his artifacts, flints which are thought to be strike-a-lights are occasionally found. These tools have edges which are polished from being struck repeatedly against crystals of iron pyrites to give a shower of sparks for kindling fire. It is thought that this method of making fire may have been discovered when sparks were accidentally produced when a piece of iron pyrites was used as a hammer stone. Other methods of starting fire, for example rubbing wood together until the heat of friction caused combustion, were also known to early man.

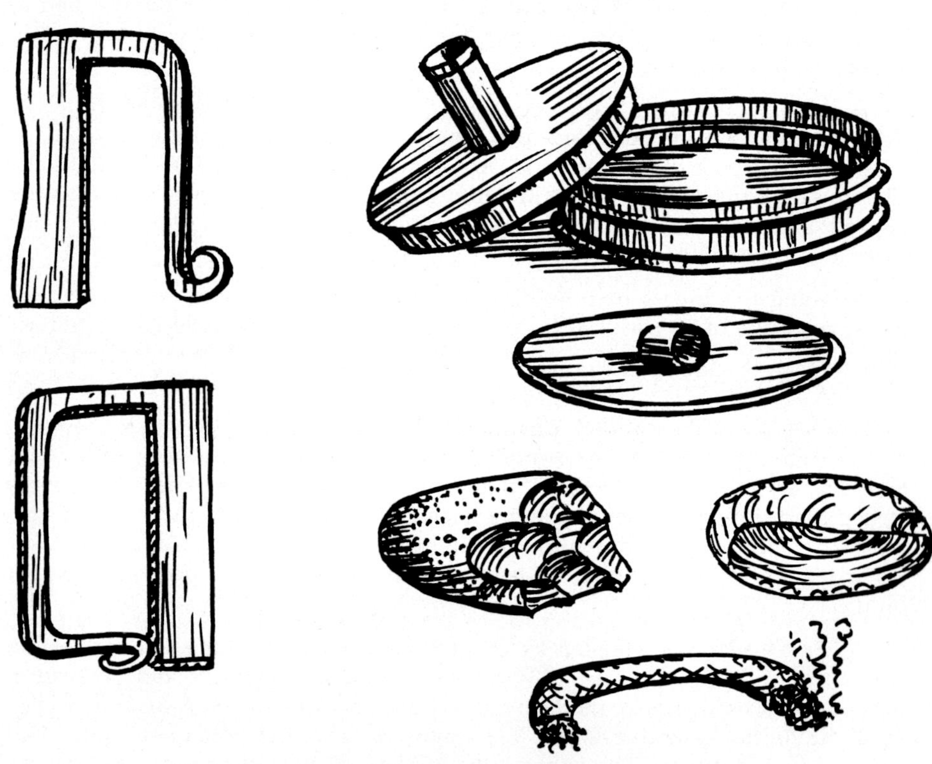

Tinder box with candle holder. The inner lid was used to cover and extinguish the smouldering tinder. The flint and steel were stored above the inner lid

In various parts of the world for many centuries, strike-a-lights were the principal means of starting fire. After the discovery of iron, it was usual to use a piece of flint and strike it on a piece of iron shaped to be held across the knuckles. The sparks were directed towards any very dry material or tinder which could be ignited and then carefully nursed into flame by very gentle blowing. Sulphur matches (made by dipping pieces of wood, cardboard or fibre into molten sulphur) were sometimes used. When a sulphur match was applied to the smouldering tinder it ignited easily.

Tinder could be obtained in many ways. Pieces of linen teased out and charred, fibre from stems of plants beaten to make them fine, and various species of polyporous or corkwood fungus were all used for this purpose.

It was usual to carry the steel, flint and tinder in a container called a 'tinder box'. This box sometimes incorporated a candlestick on the lid but was often only a small wooden box or tin which could be carried around in a pocket.

In some countries the use of strike-a-lights for lighting candles became of religious significance. On Maundy Thursday it was customary to extinguish the candles and to relight them with new fire. 'At the ninth hour a fire is produced by a flint and steel, sufficient to light a candle. A lamp lighted from this is kept unextinguished in the Church until Easter Eve to light the Pascal taper which is to be blessed on that day.'

Kindling fire in this way remained a tradition in some denominations until recent years. It was only in 1970 that the Roman Catholic Church permitted the use of a cigarette lighter for lighting the Pascal candle. It should be noted that the 'flint' in a cigarette lighter is manufactured from an alloy of cerium and other rare metals with iron.

Even after phosphorus matches (lucifers) were introduced in 1832, strike-a-lights remained in common use for many years.

During the late 17th century explosions in coal mines caused considerable damage and loss of life. It was known that the candle used by the miners ignited the fire-damp but there was no alternative method of lighting until Carlisle Spedding invented the 'steel mill'. He had observed that although fire-damp could be readily kindled by flame it was not so easily ignited in any other way. His small machine had a handle by which 'a thin disc of steel 5 or 6 inches in diameter was made to rotate at great velocity, and on a piece of flint being applied to the edge of the revolving disc a continuous flow of brilliant sparks was emitted, sufficient to enable the miners to carry on their work in places where the use of candles could on no account be allowed.' The steel mill, which was probably invented about 1740, was first used at Whitehaven. It was supported on legs with curved padded bases so that it could be strapped to a boy's left forearm, while the handle was turned with his right hand.

In 1785, after two explosions at the Wallsend Colliery, the safety of the steel mill was first brought into doubt. After two more explosions the miners' self-confidence was shaken to such an extent that they were prepared to work in feeble light rather than use their steel mills. In desperation they even tried to get light from decaying fish in a phosphorescent condition but were not successful.

In spite of its known insecurity, the steel mill continued to be used in those mines where candles were inadmissible until the safety lamp was invented in 1815 by Sir Humphrey Davy. At this time, at Hebburn Colliery alone, at least 100 steel mills were in daily use.

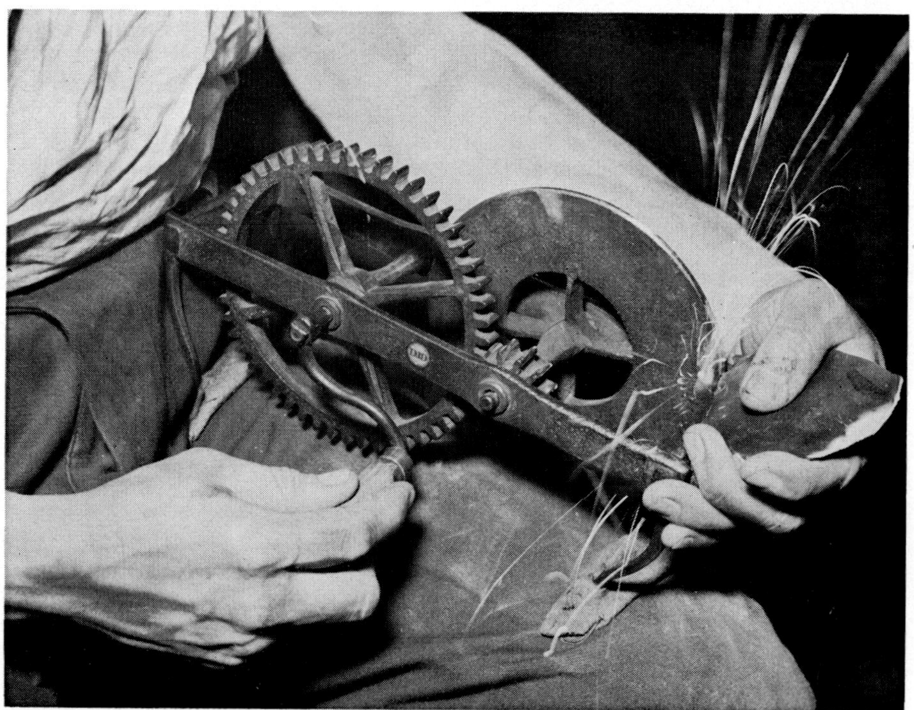

Photo Crown Copyright] [*Science Museum, London*

Miner's steel mill—demonstrating how it was operated

A FIGHTING *Chance*

Overcoming the Academic and Domestic Struggles
of Children in Foster Care

DR. BRITTANY BUSH